Elementary - Early Intermediate

THE BIG & EASY

T0014946

CHRISTMAS SONGBOOK FOR UKULELE WITH TABLATURE

Compiled and arranged by Philip Groeber

Welcome to the *The Big & Easy Christmas Songbook for Ukulele with Tablature*! You are holding in your hand a unique collection of music that is easy to learn, fun to play, and specifically selected for beginning students of the ukulele.

At first glance you might not recognize some of the song titles, but once you get out your ukulele and start playing the melodies and strumming the chords, you will be surprised and excited that you can now play so many familiar songs. That's the great part about having your own music books: you can learn old and new songs on your own!

Included are American and International Holiday songs arranged for ukulele solos or duets. Enjoy the songs that you want to play at home, with your friends, or at public appearances such as recitals and festivals. For easy use, all of the songs are listed in three ways: alphabetically, by level of difficulty, and by genre. Any way you look at it, you can quickly find the exact song you want.

Features:

- **Newly engraved music** with standard notation, tab staff with rhythm indications, chord fingerboard diagrams at every chord change, and lyrics when applicable

- **Get Familiar with the Music** provides interesting background material for every song in the book

- **Strumming Page** gives you strumming and fingerpicking tips along with 12 strum patterns including **YouTube videos**

- **Chord Fingerboard Diagrams** are included for every chord change

- **Glossary** helps you to understand many musical terms and symbols

- **Chords Used in this Book** chart that contains all 44 chord voicings

- **More About Your Ukulele** learn about ukulele campanella style and other interesting tips

THE
F·J·H
MUSIC
COMPANY
INC.
Frank J. Hackinson

Production: Frank J. Hackinson
Production Coordinator: Philip Groeber
Cover Design: Andi Whitmer
Engraving: Tempo Music Press, Inc.
Printer: Tempo Music Press, Inc.

ISBN-13: 978-1-61928-277-3

Song Titles*

Alphabetical

* The alphabetical song order is slightly altered inside the book to eliminate unwanted page turns.

Performing with Others

For maximum musical enjoyment and all-around fun, play the music in this book with others.

• All songs can be performed as duets
  a) play (or sing) the melody while someone else strums the chords
  b) without stopping, start strumming the chords as someone else plays (or sings) the melody
• Invite other musicians to join in, guitarists, pianists, bass players, vocalists, and all others are always welcome
• Record your ensemble and share the recording with others.

Level of Difficulty

Elementary Level

Basic Rhythms; First Position

Rhythm 1 ♫, ♩.; Accidentals, Various Positions

Rhythm 2 Late Elementary

Intermediate Level

Higher Positions

The following factors were considered in arranging the melodies by level of difficulty.

- rhythm
- note range
- recognizable melody
- song length
- use of accidentals
- techniques required

Use the list on this page as an approximate guide, every performer has different strengths. The level of difficulty for the harmony (strumming or fingerpicking the chords), will vary from song to song.

Get Familiar with the Music

A la nanita nana
This Spanish carol is more than 300 years old.

Angels from the Realms of Glory
Englishman, James Montgomery, wrote the lyrics in 1816 and a few years later a London organist, Henry Smart, provided the melody.

Angels We Have Heard on High
The melody is fun to play! The chords, however, sometimes change on every beat; at a joyful tempo. So, get ready!

As with Gladness Men of Old
The lyrics were written by Englishman William Chatterton Dix while he was bedridden with a serious illness. This song contains many of the most commonly used chords for the ukulele. However, they change on almost every beat!

Auld Lang Syne
Be prepared to perform this song at the stroke of midnight on New Year's Eve! This tradition started in Scotland many years ago and has since spread to countries all over the world.

Away in a Manger
This tender melody in 3/4 time is one of the most beautiful Christmas carols.

Bring a Torch, Jeanette, Isabella
This beautiful song tells the story of a French Christmas Eve custom where the villagers would light the path to the manger scene using torches. I wonder who Jeanette and Isabella were …

Chanukah
The story of Chanukah tells of the miracle of a small amount of oil that lasted for eight days.

Christmas Bells (Round)
This carol is written in a musical style called a **round**.
To perform as a round, you need at least two players, but three is best.
Player 1 begins as usual at letter A. Player 2 begins from the beginning of the song (A) as Player 1 gets to B. Player 3 begins from the beginning of the song as Player 1 gets to C. Play as long as you wish. If Player 3 ends up playing the last two measures alone, then everything worked out perfectly!

The Coventry Carol
Tell your friends that this English carol features a Picardy third; they will then know that you are a very knowledgable ukulele player! This term means that the song is in a minor key, as this song is in the key of A minor. On the final chord the composer may sometimes unexpectedly insert a major chord, in this case A major. Some people refer to this as, "the happy third." Try this technique on a song of your choice.

Deck the Halls
A Welsh melody which was written in the 16th century. Sometimes the title appears as *Deck the Hall*.

Ding, Dong! Merrily on High
This carol shares a popular treatment of the lyric "Gloria," with the carol *Angels We Have Heard on High*. Both carols elongate the syllable "O" over many measures. This technique is referred to as a "melismatic melody sequence."

G1074

The Dreidel Song
A dreidel is a four-sided top that is played by children during Chanukah.

Fingerpicking Fun
Memorize this eighth-note fingerpicking pattern and use it on many of the songs in this book.

The First Noel
An 18th-century English Christmas carol that describes the Nativity of Jesus. The melody of this song is based on the C major scale, so again your time spent practicing scales will pay off. Get ready to change chords on almost every beat!

Go, Tell it on the Mountain
Dating back to the early 1800s, this popular Christmas song is an African-American spiritual. It has been sung and recorded by many gospel and secular performers. Here is a list of recent recordings: Blues Traveler, Hanson, Pentatonix, and Sarah McLachlan.

God Rest Ye Merry, Gentlemen
This song, first published in 1827, was chosen by the author Charles Dickens to be included in his famous book, *A Christmas Carol.* This is another song that was sung by the Waits in old London. See the text for *We Wish You a Merry Christmas.*

Good Christian Men, Rejoice!
This song is in 6/8 time, so there are 6 beats in a measure, but an *eighth note* receives 1 beat. So, all the quarter notes get 2 beats, and the dotted quarters get 3 beats. It is easier to count only 2 beats in a measure, with each beat having 3 parts.

Good King Wenceslas
The melody of this song is over 800 years old. The lyrics tell a story about a Bohemian prince who was very kind and spent a lot of his time and money helping the poor.

Goodnight (Round)
See *Christmas Bells* text describing a round. Can you play and sing at the same time? I think so.

Hark! The Herald Angels Sing
This joyful theme by Felix Mendelssohn features 10 different chords! Hark! Are you ready?

He Is Born the Holy Child
This traditional French carol was first published in the late 1800s. Be sure to exaggerate the tempo changes in the last four measures.

Hey, Ho, Nobody Home (Round)
See *Christmas Bells* text describing a round. This popular round dates back to England in the 16th century. At that time there were groups of Christmas carolers singing door to door, anticipating food and drink in exchange for their harmony.

The Holly and the Ivy
The symbolism in this ancient carol is the representation of holly as Jesus, and the ivy as His mother, Mary. As a musician, you may notice that the harmony of the song only uses the Primary Chords in the Key of G major: G, C, and D7.

Hope It's Santa
This original Christmas song is a lot of fun to play as a duet because the notes and the chords can easily be played by beginning ukulele players of all ages. If at all possible, add percussion instruments. Sleigh bells can be used throughout the entire song. Add a vibraslap or clapper on beat 1 in measures 9, 11, and 13 for an ear-catching sound!

I Got the Blues (For Christmas)
You will learn a lot about the 12-Bar Blues with this song, "Could ol' Santa have forgotten me?"

I Heard the Bells on Christmas Day
The renowned American author, Henry Wadsworth Longfellow, wrote these beautiful lyrics during the Civil War after his son was severely wounded in the conflict. His lyrics proclaim that "right" shall prevail, bringing peace and goodwill to all, provided there is Christmas and its promise of new life.

I Saw Three Ships
This traditional English carol was written around 1666. No one is sure exactly what the three ships refer to. There are those who say they are the Three Wise Men. Some say they are perhaps the three virtues of faith, hope, and charity, while others suggest they are the members of the Holy Family.

It Came Upon the Midnight Clear
This carol was composed in Massachusetts in the year 1849. This melody is played in the Key of A.

Jesu, Joy of Man's Desiring
This is one of the recognizable melodies ever written by Johann Sebastian Bach. The melody consists of eighth-note triplets. Each group of three notes is played in the time of one beat.

Jingle Bells
Jingle Bells is probably the most often recorded Christmas song of all time. The lyric "two forty" in the 4th verse refers to the speed of the horse, dashing a mile in 2 minutes and 40 seconds!

Jolly Old Saint Nicholas
St. Nicholas was a bishop from Greece who had a reputation for secret gift giving. The modern day Santa Claus is somewhat based on his life.

Joy to the World
One of the most revered of all Christmas carols, the opening melody is easily identified by a descending major scale. All of the hours you have spent practicing scales will pay off in this arrangement!

Let All Mortal Flesh Keep Silence
This beautiful melody is greatly enhanced by its harmony, that is the chords of the song.

Lo, How a Rose E'er Blooming
This German melody has a very interesting chord progression, and there are *many* chord changes. Spend time practicing the chords carefully so you do not miss a beat. Play the melody with a slow, solemn feel with a lot of expression (bending the tempo).

Lullaby, Jesus
This is a beautiful sounding melody when performed on a ukulele. Play softly and gently.

March (from *The Nutcracker Suite*)
This Tchaikovsky favorite spends a lot of time in the higher positions on the ukulele.

O Christmas Tree
This is one of the merriest of all Christmas carols! The German word *Tannenbaum* is a fir tree. The song is more about an actual fir tree rather than a Christmas tree.

O Come, All Ye Faithful
Known by the Latin title, *Adeste Fidelis*, the melody of this Christmas carol is sometimes attributed to John Wade or John Reading back in the 1700s.

O Come, Little Children
The lyrics to this carol relate the story of Christmas in a very special way to young children.
When practicing the chords, spend extra time changing from Dm to B♭.

O Come, O Come Emmanuel
Play this Advent song slowly, flowing and free. In order to insure a dramatic performance, exaggerate contrasts in volume by closely following the dynamics that are indicated.

O Holy Night
This well-known Christmas carol was composed by the Frenchman, Adolphe Adam, in 1847. Practice the melody slowly and carefully, be as accurate as possible.

O Little Town of Bethlehem
The lyricist, Philip Brooks, was inspired to write the words to this famous carol after a visit to the Holy Land in 1868. The organist at his church, Louis Redner, later wrote the melody.

Once in David's Royal City
This song, usually performed in Advent, is a song about Bethlehem. This beautiful melody has many chord changes. Begin playing a slower tempo in order to strum the chords exactly as written.

Over the River and Through the Wood
This song was originally performed as a song to be sung at Thanksgiving. Recent research has found that to be correct, the last word of the title is "wood", not "woods."

Parade of the Wooden Soldiers
This melody, originally written as a novelty dance song, eventually was included in a Broadway show, *The Bat*, in 1922. There are lyrics to this melody, but they are seldom used today. The appealing melody and rhythm of this song, along with the term "wooden soldiers" in the title, helped the song to become a Christmas favorite. This arrangement contains many open strings which makes the campanella style ring out!

Ring Little Bells
This German carol has always been a song that is popular with handbell choirs.

Rocking Carol
This carol, first published in 1920 in Czechoslovakia, was very popular at the time, but became obscure in the following years. Singer/actress, Julie Andrews, made a well-received recording in the 1960s, and so the popularity of this carol is still growing.

Silent Night
In 1818, Joseph Mohr brought his lyrics to Franz Gruber and asked him to write a melody for his new song, *Stille Nacht* (Silent Night). Franz wrote an arrangement for voice and guitar—the rest is history.

Sing We Now of Christmas
This Christmas carol was originally intended to be sung on New Year's Day. The melody of this carol is in the Dorian Mode. This mode is similar to the E minor scale, but the sixth note of the scale is raised one half-step higher (C♯), giving the melody more drive and adding brightness to the scale.

Skaters' Waltz
The composer, Émile Waldteufel, is known as the *Waltz King of France*, mainly because he wrote over 250 waltz tunes. He wrote *Skaters' Waltz* when ice skating was the fashionable craze in France, and to this day you will hear this melody played at the ice (or roller) skating rink of your choice.

Toyland
This song was written by Victor Herbert in 1903, taken from his operetta *Babes in Toyland*. In 1997 an animated movie of *Babes in Toyland* was released by MGM, based on the operetta.

The Twelve Days of Christmas
To make this song an even more fun event with a group of people, prepare 11 cards, each one marked with one of the days of Christmas (except the fifth day). Pass these cards out before you begin playing and have everyone with a card sing the lyrics for their day, by themselves. Everybody sings on, "Five gold rings!" Good times!

Ukrainian Bell Carol
This melody written in 1914 is more widely known as the *Carol of the Bells* after appearing in the movie *Home Alone*, and recorded by many popular groups such as: Mannheim Steamroller, The Muppets, and Pentatonix. Practice the hammer-on technique used throughout this arrangement.

Up on the Housetop
This song, written by Benjamin Hanby of Ohio around the year 1864, is one of the first songs that suggested that Santa's sleigh could actually land on a rooftop! This arrangement contains many open strings which makes the campanella style ring out!

We Three Kings of Orient Are
John Henry Hopkins wrote this song, probably the most popular song about the Three Wise Men, in New York City in 1857. If someone asks you "What are the names of the Three Kings?" you say, "Melchior, Caspar, and Balthazar."

We Wish You a Merry Christmas
This happy Christmas song originated in England at a time when music was the main attraction in most villages. Groups of singers, called Waits, would be singing day and night during the Christmas season. After singing rousing choruses of songs like *We Wish You a Merry Christmas,* they were often rewarded by receiving gifts of money or fig pudding. See the text for *God Rest Ye Merry, Gentlemen.*

Wexford Carol
This very old carol originated in County Wexford, Ireland. The combination of an unusual 3/4 rhythm and interesting chord changes make this a fun piece to play. Investigate this song in more detail by listening to recent recordings by Yo Yo Ma with Alison Krauss, Irish folksinger Cara Dillon, and the Irish group Celtic Women.

What Child Is This
There is a rumor, persistent to this day, that this melody was written by King Henry VIII of England for his future wife, Anne Boleyn. The same melody is also used for the English folksong *Greensleeves*.

While Shepherds Watched Their Flocks
This is a medley of two versions of the story of the shepherds on Christmas Day. The arrangement begins in the Key of F with the Nathan Tate song which originated in England in the 1700s. The second part of the arrangement, in the Key of C, was written by George Frideric Handel in his 1728 opera *Siroe*. This version is the one most commonly used in the United States.

Strumming Page

Strumming Tips:

- If you are just beginning to play the ukulele, you may want to get started using a **Thumb Strum**. Place your thumb on the 4th string (G) around the area where the neck of your uke meets the body. Gently strum downwards towards the floor. This is called a downstroke (⊓). To help support your ukulele when using the Thumb Strum, you may want to cradle your R.H. fingers around the bottom of the uke for stability.

- Strumming with your index finger is a very popular way to strum the ukulele and is the strum that you should learn next. With a loose wrist, use the nail of your index finger to strum down, being sure to play all four strings. When using an upstrum (∨), use the fleshy part of your finger. For more strumming details, check out the YouTube videos featuring Ukulele Mike discussing various ukulele strums: **fjhmusic.com/g1055/page10**

- Even though it is not indicated, you may add a final strum at the end of some of the pieces. Strum a chord on beat 1 after the last measure. Let it ring!

- If a strum is too difficult to play, go back to a basic strum. Basic strums always work well.

- The recommended strums can always be substituted for another; use the one that you like the best.

- In 4/4 time when there are two chords in a measure they will usually be strummed on beats 1 and 3. However, you will always need to look at the location of the chord names over the melody notes to find the *exact* beat on which the chords change.

Fingerpicking Tips:

The right-hand fingers are identified by letter name only: thumb (*t*), index (*i*), and middle (*m*). Accent the first note to help you keep track of beat 1, keep a very steady pulse. Begin using only open strings as shown, then fingerpick a few chords. When you are ready, start fingerpicking your favorite songs!

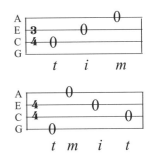

Strum Patterns

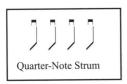

Quarter-Note Strum

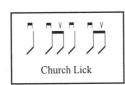

Church Lick

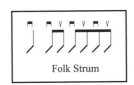

Folk Strum

Calypso Strum

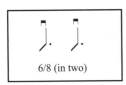

6/8 (in two)

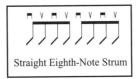

Straight Eighth-Note Strum

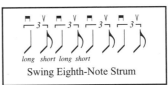

long short long short
Swing Eighth-Note Strum

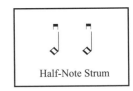

Half-Note Strum

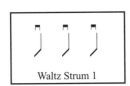

Waltz Strum 1

Waltz Strum 2

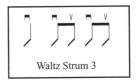

Waltz Strum 3

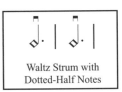

Waltz Strum with Dotted-Half Notes

Specialized Strum Pattern

This strum is recommended to use when the chord changes are in an unusual rhythm pattern. Strum one time for each indicated chord, but also strum on beat 1 of every measure, even though a chord may not be indicated. In this case use the last chord in the previous measure.

Suggested strumming patterns are indicated for every piece but feel free to substitute a different strum from the list above at any time. You may want to create your own strums.

Music Notation Page

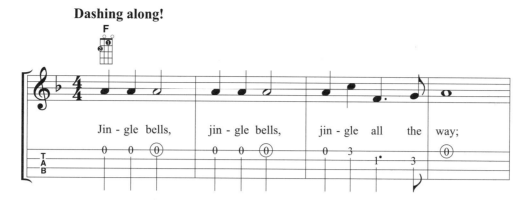

Dashing along!

Jin - gle bells, | jin - gle bells, | jin - gle all the way;

Music in this book will contain both a five-line staff using standard notation and a four-line TAB staff.

The music staff is in treble clef and is able to be used by the ukulele as well as flute, guitar, piano, recorder, and violin. Other instruments such as clarinet, saxophone, and trumpet can also play but will need to transpose the music to be in the same key as the music is written. Chord names/frames and lyrics are included.

The four-line TAB staff is a very helpful tool that shows you the exact location of the notes by string (the horizontal lines) and the fret (the numbers ON the line). In addition, this book also shows the rhythm in the TAB staff.

Ukulele Fingerboard Chart
This chart shows you where to place your fingers for the various chords used in the book. In this chart the strings are vertical lines with the 1st string (A, the thinnest string) on the right side of the chart.
The numbers inside the circles indicate where to place your fingers.
x = do not play this string, o = play this open string

The chords written inside the staff may not always match the chord charts shown above the staff.

Natural Notes

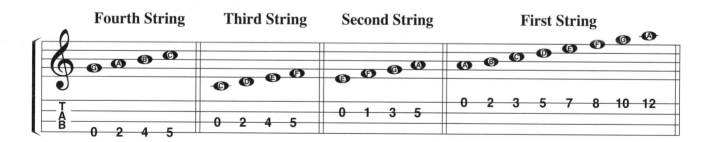

Fourth String | Third String | Second String | First String

Key Signatures
Major and Relative Minor Keys

Key of C (Am)
no sharps or flats

Key of G (Em)
F♯

Key of D (Bm)
F♯, C♯

Key of A (F♯m)
F♯, C♯, G♯

Key of F (Dm)
B♭

A LA NANITA NANA
TRADITIONAL SPANISH CAROL

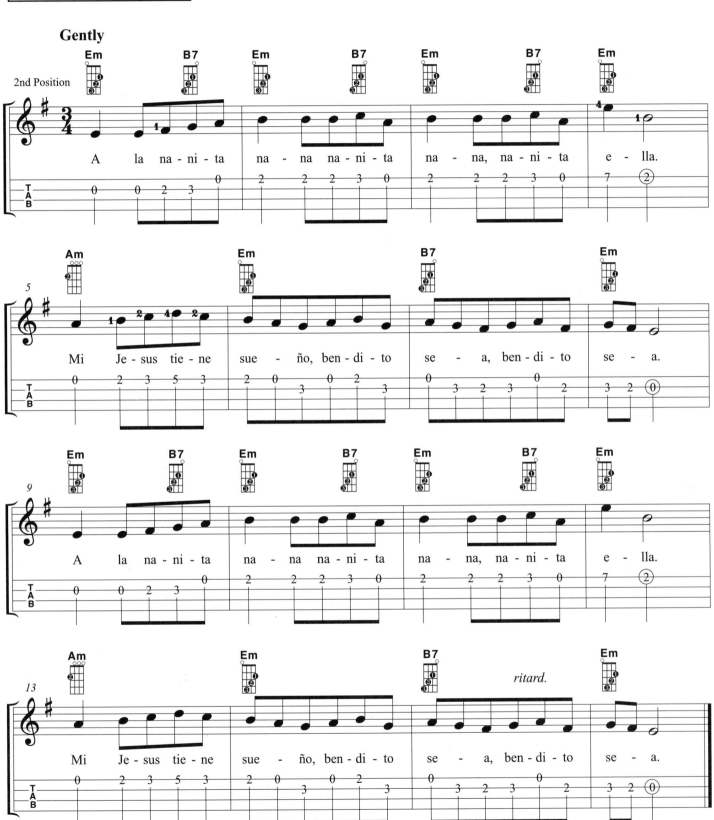

ANGELS FROM THE REALMS OF GLORY

LYRICS BY JAMES MONTGOMERY
MUSIC BY HENRY SMART

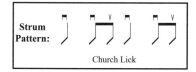

ANGELS WE HAVE HEARD ON HIGH

TRADITIONAL FRENCH CAROL

As with Gladness Men of Old

Lyrics by William Chatterton Dix
Music by Conrad Kocher

Specialized Strum
(see page 10)

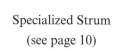

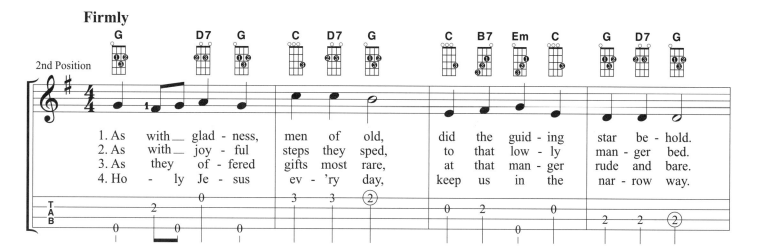

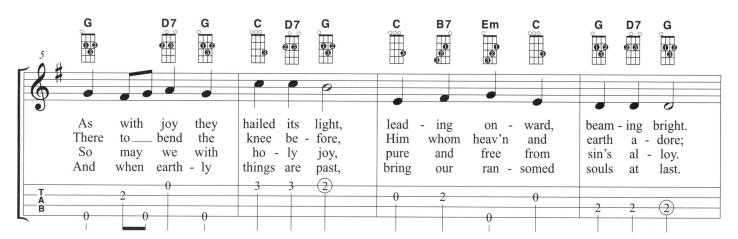

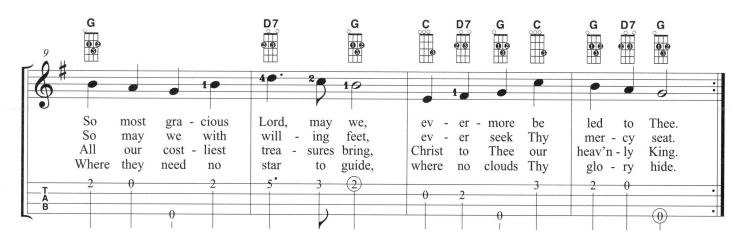

AULD LANG SYNE

OLD LONG SINCE

LYRICS BY ROBERT BURNS
TRADITIONAL SCOTTISH MELODY

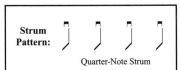

Away in a Manger

LYRICS TRADITIONAL
MUSIC BY JAMES R. MURRAY

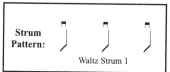

BRING A TORCH, JEANETTE, ISABELLA

TRADITIONAL PROVENÇAL CAROL
LYRICS TRANSLATED BY CUTHBERT NUNN

CHANUKAH

TRADITIONAL

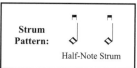

Happily

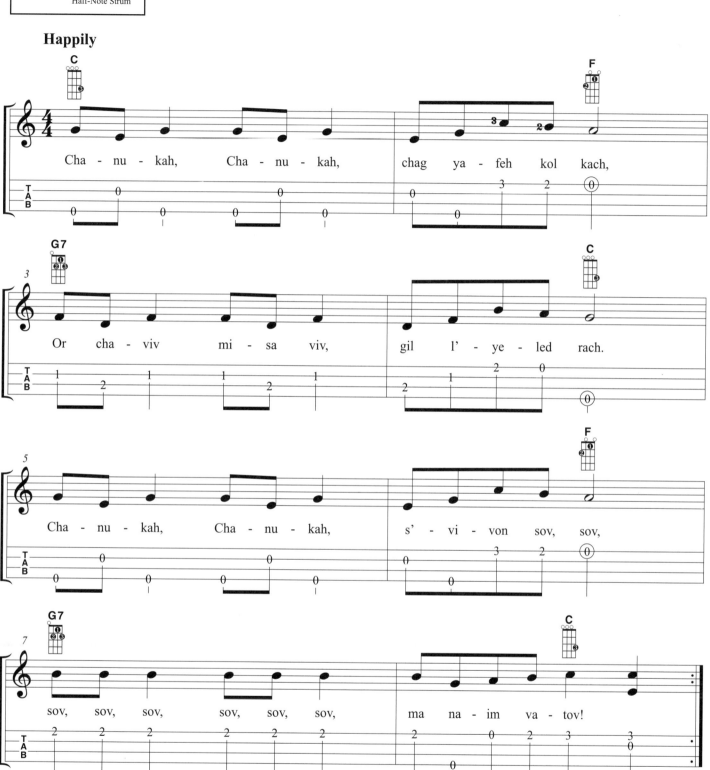

CHRISTMAS BELLS
ROUND

TRADITIONAL GERMAN FOLKSONG

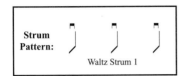

THE COVENTRY CAROL

LULLAY, THOU LITTLE TINY CHILD
LYRICS ATTRIBUTED TO ROBERT CROO
ANCIENT ENGLISH CAROL

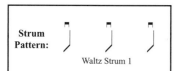

Strum Pattern:

Waltz Strum 1

Slowly

2nd Position

1. Lul - lay, thou lit - tle ti - ny child,
2. O sis - ters too, how may we do,

bye, bye, lul - ly lu - lay; Lul -
for to pre - serve this day? This

lay, thou lit - tle ti - ny child.
poor young - ling for whom we sing.

Bye, bye, lul - ly, lul - lay.
Bye, bye, lul - ly, lul - lay.

G1074

Deck the Halls

Traditional Welsh Air

Ding Dong! Merrily on High

Lyrics by George Ratcliffe Woodward
French Folk Melody

2. E'en so here below, below,
   let steeple bells be swungen;
   And "Io, io, io!"
   By priest and people sungen.

3. Pray you, dutifully prime,
   your matin chime, ye ringers;
   May you beautifully rime,
   Your eve time song, ye singers.

THE DREIDEL SONG

TRADITIONAL

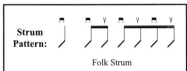

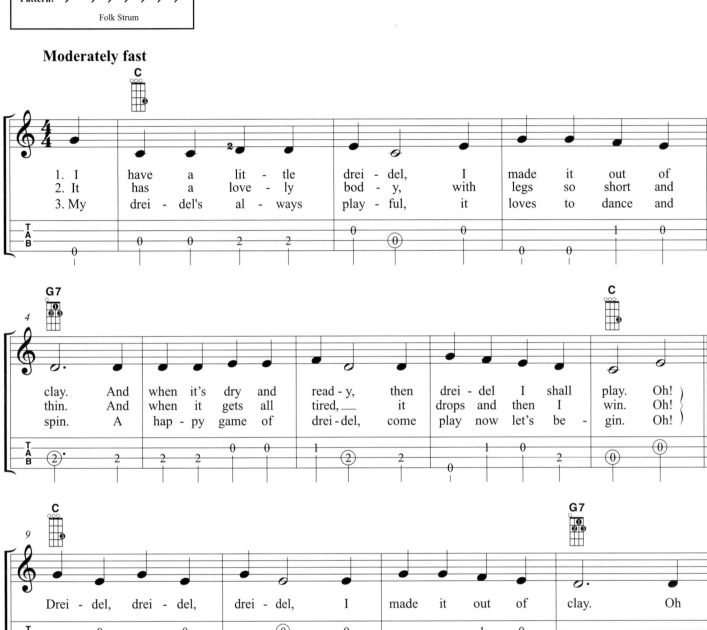

Go, Tell It on the Mountain

African-American Spiritual

With joy! *(swing the eighth notes)*

2. The shepherds feared and trembled,
   when lo! above the earth.
   Rang out the angel chorus,
   that hailed our Saviour's birth.

3. Down in a lowly manger,
   our humble Christ was born.
   And God send us salvation,
   that blessed Christmas morn.

THE FIRST NOEL

TRADITIONAL ENGLISH AIR

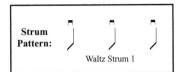

3. And by the light of that same star,
   Three Wise men came from country far.
   To seek for a King was their intent,
   and to follow the star wherever it went.
   Noel, Noel, Noel, Noel!
   Born is the King of Israel!

FINGERPICKING FUN

Practice this fingerpicking pattern on the ending to *Jingle Bells*
and then you will soon be dashing off to even more Christmas classics!

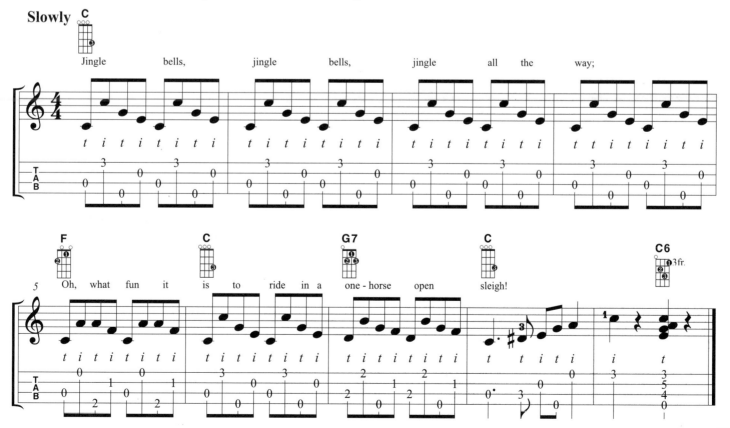

God Rest Ye Merry, Gentlemen

Traditional English Carol

GOOD CHRISTIAN MEN, REJOICE!

IN DULCI JUBILO
LYRICS TRANSLATED BY JOHN MASON NEALE
GERMAN HYMN

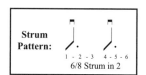

Good King Wenceslas

Lyrics by James Mason Neale
Traditional

Specialized Strum
(see page 10)

GOODNIGHT
ROUND
TRADITIONAL

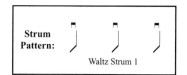

Moderately

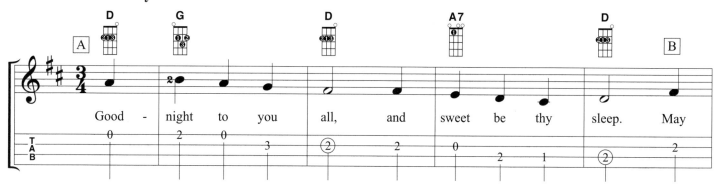

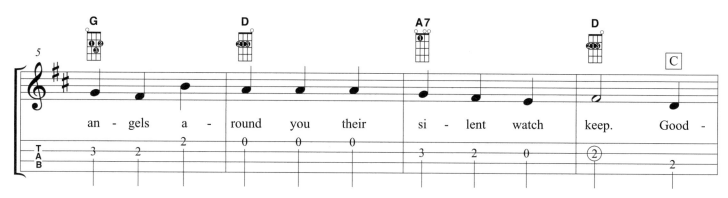

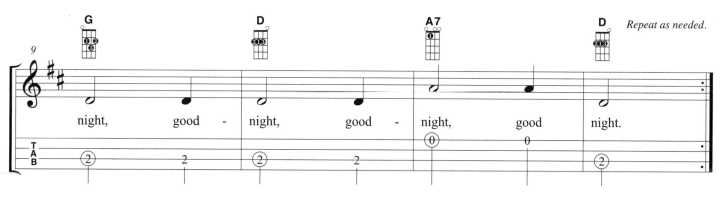

Hark! The Herald Angels Sing

Lyrics by Charles Wesley
Music by Felix Mendelssohn; Adapted by William Cummings

HE IS BORN, THE HOLY CHILD

IL EST NÉ, LE DIVIN ENFANT
TRADITIONAL FRENCH CAROL

HEY, HO, NOBODY HOME
ROUND
TRADITIONAL ENGLISH

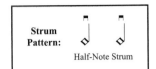

THE HOLLY AND THE IVY

TRADITIONAL ENGLISH CAROL

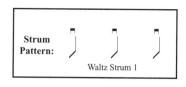

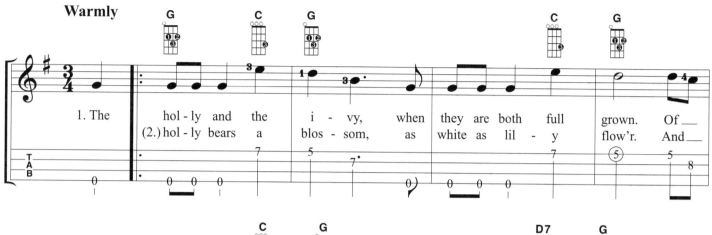

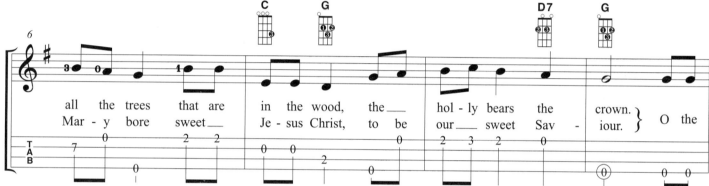

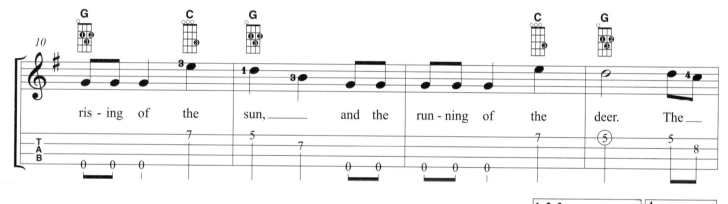

3. The holly bears a berry, as red as any blood.
   And Mary bore sweet Jesus Christ, to do poor sinners good.

4. The holly bears a prickle, as sharp as any thorn;
   And Mary bore sweet Jesus Christ, on Christmas Day in the morn.

HOPE IT'S SANTA

PHILIP GROEBER

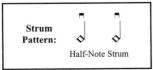

Play/sing both *Verses* 1 and 2 and then play the *Chorus* two times.

Then repeat from the beginning and play/sing *Verses* 3 and 4. Then go to the *Chorus*.

Always play the *Chorus* two times.

I Heard the Bells on Christmas Day

Lyrics by Henry Wadsworth Longfellow
Music by John Baptiste Calkin

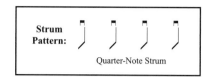

Strum Pattern:
Quarter-Note Strum

Moderately slow

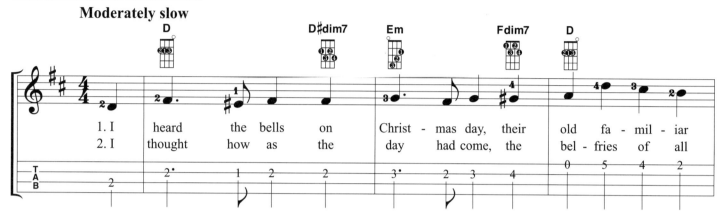

1. I heard the bells on Christ - mas day, their old fa - mil - iar
2. I thought how as the day had come, the bel - fries of all

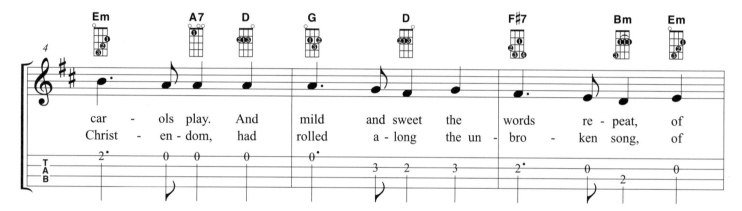

car - ols play. And mild and sweet the words re - peat, of
Christ - en - dom, had rolled a - long the un - bro - ken song, of

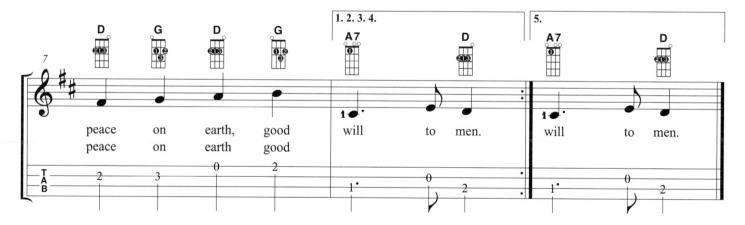

1. 2. 3. 4.

5.

peace on earth, good will to men. will to men.
peace on earth good will to men.

3. And in despair I bowed my head,
   "There is no peace on earth," I said;
   "For hate is strong and mocks the song,
   of peace on earth, good will to men."

4. Then pealed the bells more loud and deep:
   "God is not dead, nor doth He sleep;
   The wrong shall fail, the right prevail,
   with pcacc on earth, good will to men."

5. "Till ringing, singing on its way,
   the world revolved from night to day.
   A voice, a chime, a chant sublime,
   of peace on earth, good will to men."

I Got the Blues
(For Christmas)

Philip Groeber

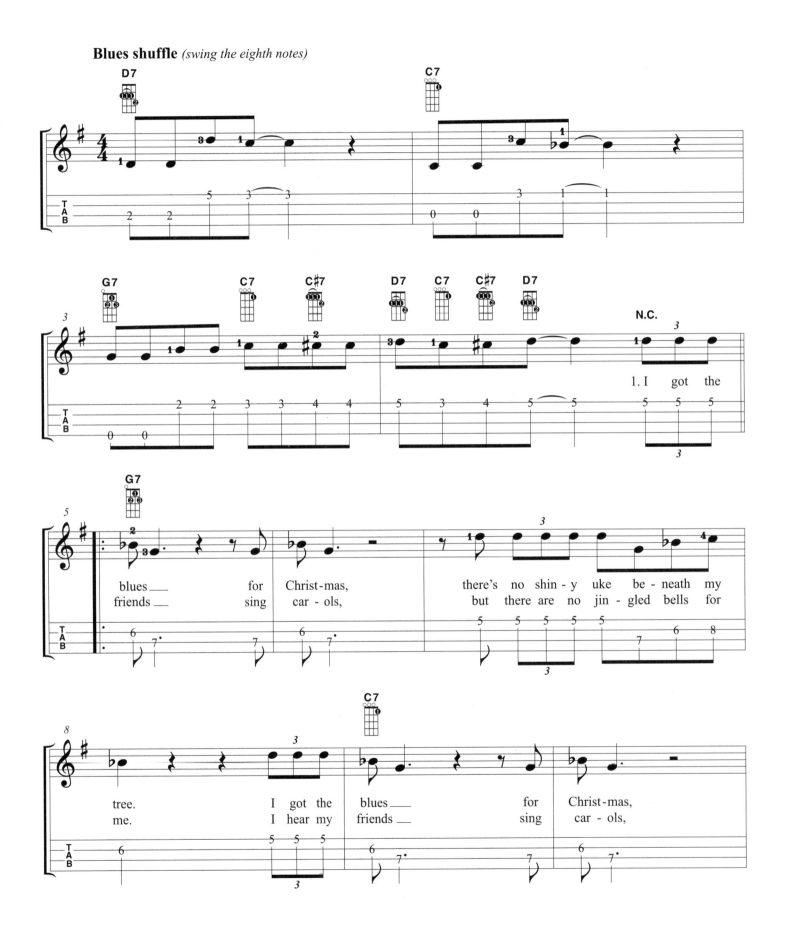

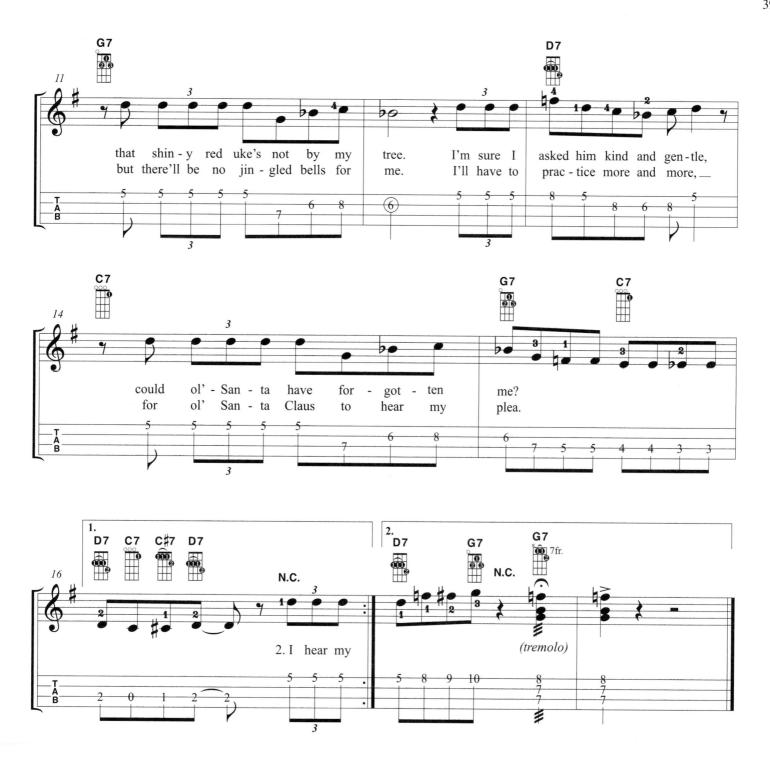

Strumming Suggestions for *I Got the Blues (For Christmas)*

The Quarter-Note Strum works well with this song.

Even better, play the Chicago Blues Riff as indicated below.

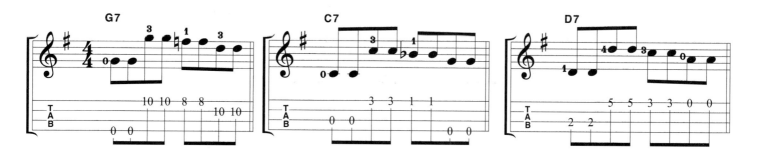

Jesu, Joy of Man's Desiring

Johann Sebastian Bach

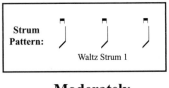

Strum Pattern:
Waltz Strum 1

Moderately

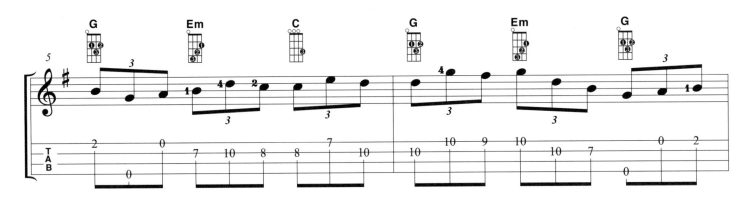

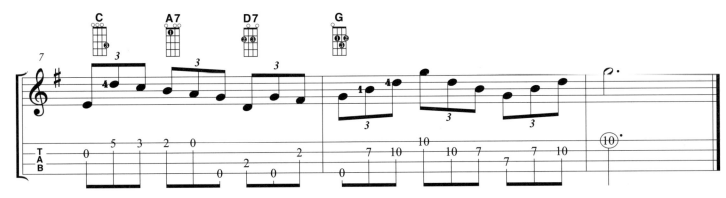

I Saw Three Ships

TRADITIONAL ENGLISH CAROL

It Came Upon the Midnight Clear

Lyrics by Edmund H. Sears
Music by Richard S. Willis

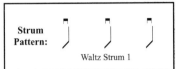

Strum Pattern: Waltz Strum 1

Peacefully

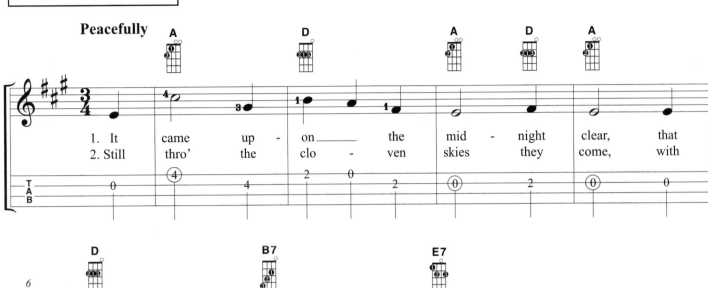

1. It came up - on the mid - night clear, that
2. Still thro' the clo - ven skies they come, that with

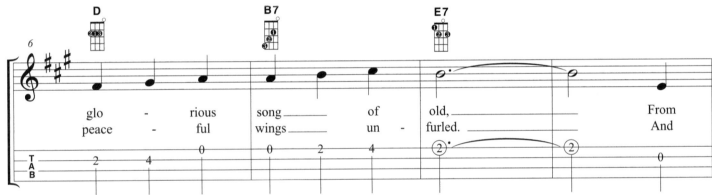

glo - rious song of old, From
peace - ful wings un - furled. And

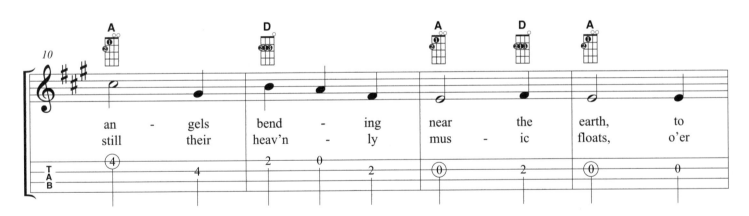

an - gels bend - ing near the earth, to
still their heav'n - ly mus - ic floats, o'er

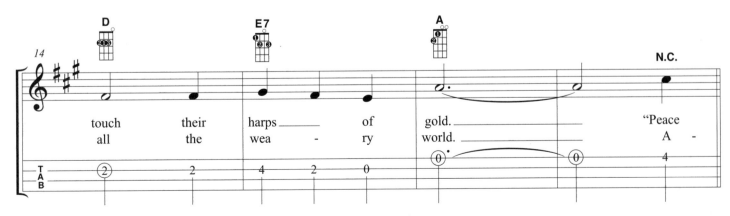

touch their harps of gold. "Peace
all the wea - ry world. A -

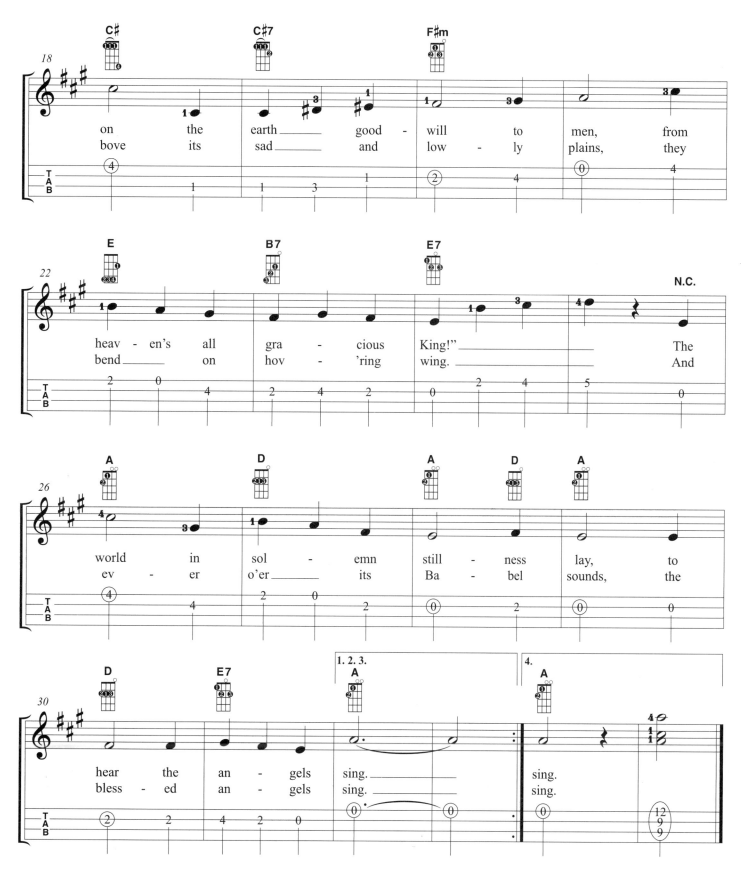

3. And ye, beneath life's crushing load,
   whose forms are bending low.
   Who toil along the climbing way,
   with painful steps and slow.
   Look now! For glad and golden hours,
   come swiftly on the wing.
   O rest beside the weary road,
   and hear the angels sing!

4. For lo! The days are hastening on,
   by prophet bards foretold.
   When with the ever-circling years,
   comes round the age of gold.
   When peace shall over all the earth,
   its ancient splendors fling.
   And the whole world give back the song,
   which now the angels sing.

Jingle Bells
James Pierpont

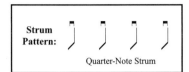

**Strum
Pattern:**

Quarter-Note Strum

Dashing along!

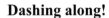

Verses:

1. Dash - ing through the snow in a one - horse o - pen sleigh;
(2.) day or two a - go, I thought I'd take a ride; and

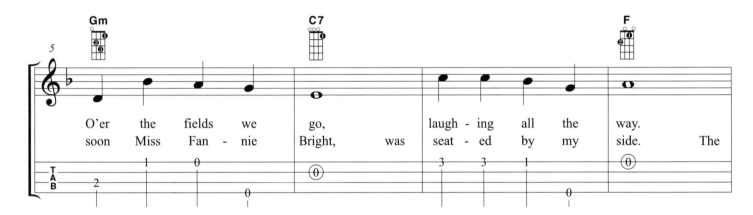

O'er the fields we go, laugh - ing all the way.
soon Miss Fan - nie Bright, was seat - ed by my side. The

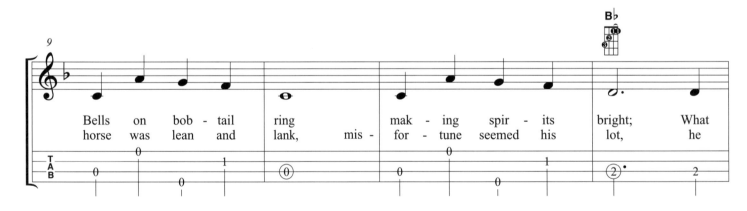

Bells on bob - tail ring, mak - ing spir - its bright; What
horse was lean and lank, mis - for - tune seemed his lot, he

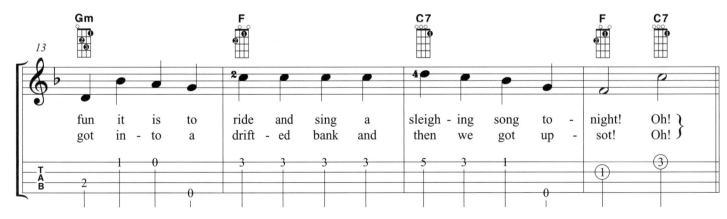

fun it is to ride and sing a sleigh - ing song to - night! Oh!
got in - to a drift - ed bank and then we got up - sot! Oh!

3. A day or two ago, the story I must tell,
   I went out on the snow, and on my back I fell.
   A gent was riding by, in a one-horse open sleigh,
   he laughed as there I sprawling lie, but quickly drove away! Oh!

4. Now the ground is white, go it while you're young.
   Take the girls tonight, and sing this sleighing song.
   Just get a bobtailed bay, two forty as his speed,
   hitch him to an open sleigh, and crack, you'll take the lead! Oh!

Jolly Old Saint Nicholas

Traditional

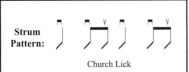

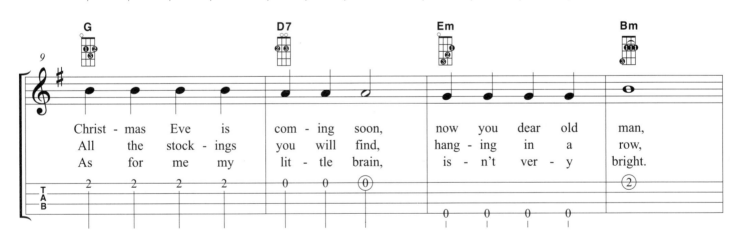

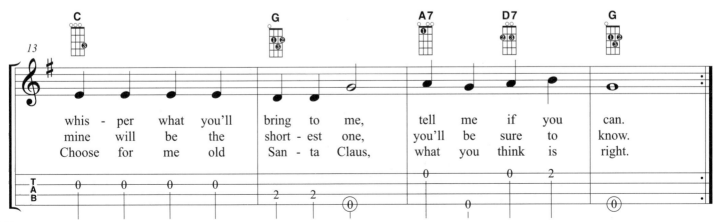

JOY TO THE WORLD

LYRICS BY ISAAC WATTS
MUSIC BY LOWELL MASON

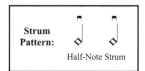

Let All Mortal Flesh Keep Silence

Lyrics from the Liturgy of St. James
Traditional French Carol

LO, HOW A ROSE E'ER BLOOMING

ES IST EIN ROS' ENTSPRUNGEN

GERMAN CAROL, MELODY HARMONIZED BY MICHAEL PRAETORIUS

Specialized Strum
(see page 10)

Lullaby, Jesus

Traditional Polish Carol

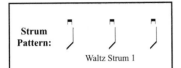

March
FROM THE NUTCRACKER SUITE
PETER ILYICH TCHAIKOVSKY

O Christmas Tree

O Tannenbaum

Small Caps: German Folksong

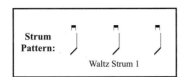

Strum Pattern: Waltz Strum 1

In a merry mood

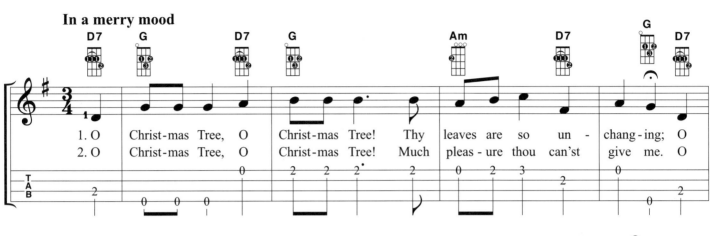

1. O Christ-mas Tree, O Christ-mas Tree! Thy leaves are so un-chang-ing; O
2. O Christ-mas Tree, O Christ-mas Tree! Much pleas-ure thou can'st give me. O

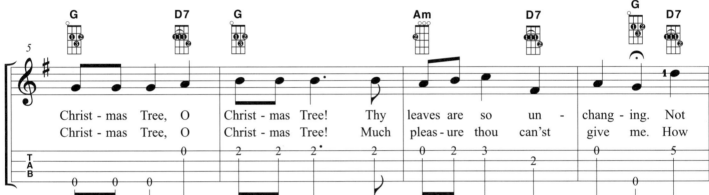

Christ-mas Tree, O Christ-mas Tree! Thy leaves are so un-chang-ing. Not
Christ-mas Tree, O Christ-mas Tree! Much pleas-ure thou can'st give me. How

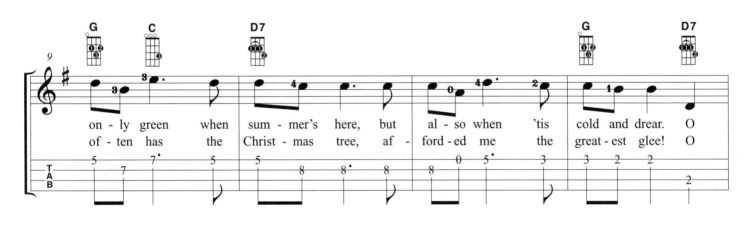

on-ly green when sum-mer's here, but al-so when 'tis cold and drear. O
of-ten has when the Christ-mas tree, af-ford-ed me the great-est glee! O

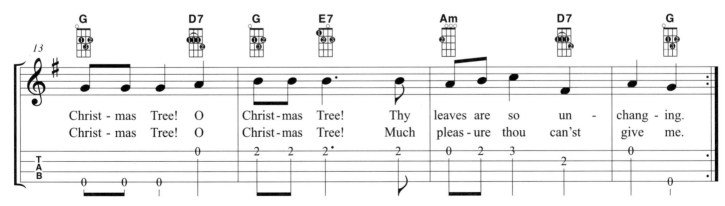

Christ-mas Tree! O Christ-mas Tree! Thy leaves are so un-chang-ing.
Christ-mas Tree! O Christ-mas Tree! Much pleas-ure thou can'st give me.

O COME, ALL YE FAITHFUL

ADESTE FIDELIS

LYRICS BY FREDERICK OAKELEY
MUSIC BY JOHN F. WADE

O Come, Little Children

LYRICS AND MUSIC BY CHRISTOPH VON SCHMID AND J. A. P. SCHULZ

O Come, O Come Emmanuel

English Lyrics by John M. Neale
Music Adapted by Thomas Helmore

O Holy Night

Cantique de Noël

French Lyrics by Placide Cappeau
Lyrics Translated by John S. Dwight
Music by Adolphe C. Adam

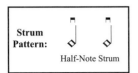

Strum Pattern:
Half-Note Strum

Slowly *(swing the eighth notes)*

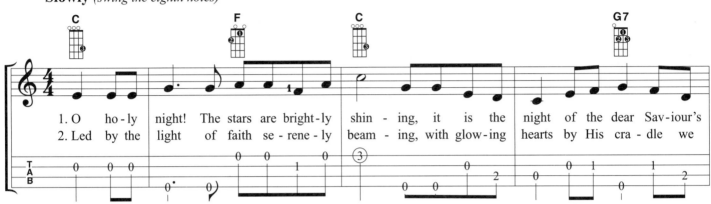

1. O ho-ly night! The stars are bright-ly shin - ing, it is the night of the dear Sav-iour's
2. Led by the light of faith se-rene-ly beam - ing, with glow-ing hearts by His cra - dle we

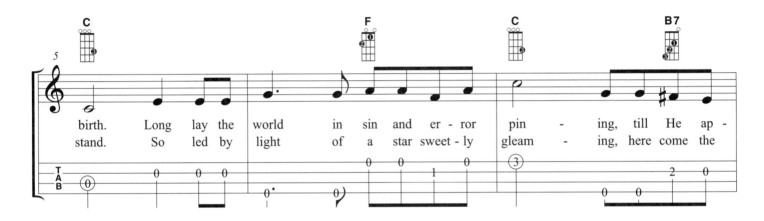

birth. Long lay the world in sin and er - ror pin - ing, till He ap -
stand. So led by light of a star sweet - ly gleam - ing, here come the

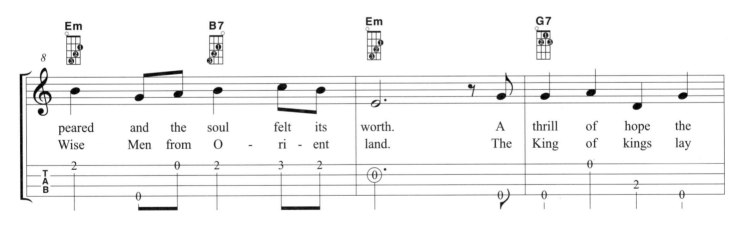

peared and the soul felt its worth. A thrill of hope the
Wise Men from O - ri - ent land. The King of kings lay

wea - ry world re - joic - es, for yon - der breaks a new and glo - rious morn.
thus in low - ly man - ger, in all our tri - als born to be our friend.

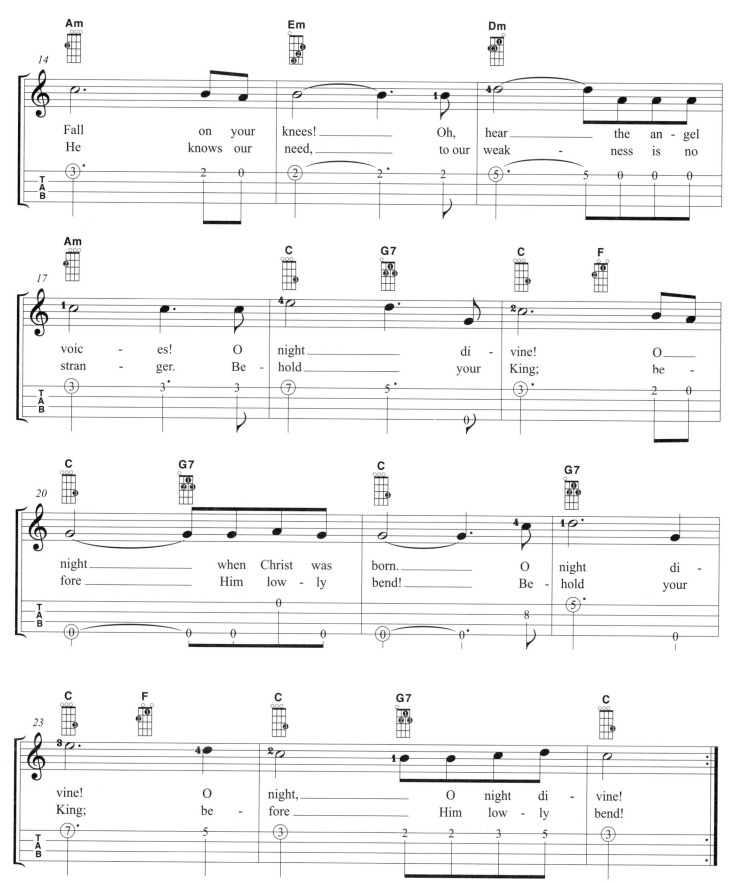

3. Truly He taught us to love one another;
His law is love and His gospel is peace.
Chains shall He break, for the slave is our brother,
and in His name all oppression shall cease.
Sweet hymns of joy in grateful chorus raise we,
let all within us praise His holy name.
Christ is the Lord; O praise His name forever!
His power and glory evermore proclaim!
His power and glory evermore proclaim!

O LITTLE TOWN OF BETHLEHEM

LYRICS BY PHILLIPS BROOKS
MUSIC BY LOUIS H. REDNER

Strum Pattern: Quarter-Note Strum

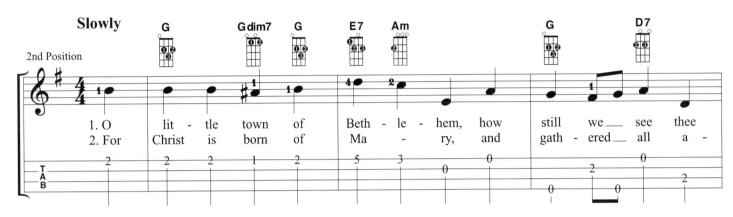

1. O lit - tle town of Beth - le - hem, how still we ___ see thee
2. For Christ is born of Ma - ry, and gath - ered ___ all a -

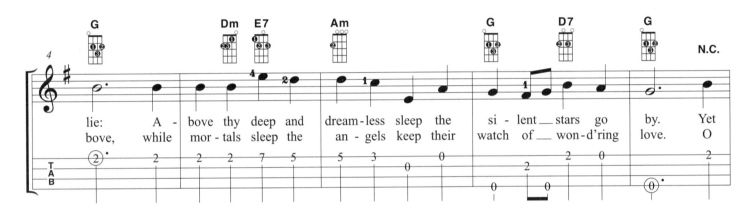

lie: A - bove thy deep and dream-less sleep the si - lent ___ stars go by. Yet
bove, while mor - tals sleep the an - gels keep their watch of ___ won - d'ring love. O

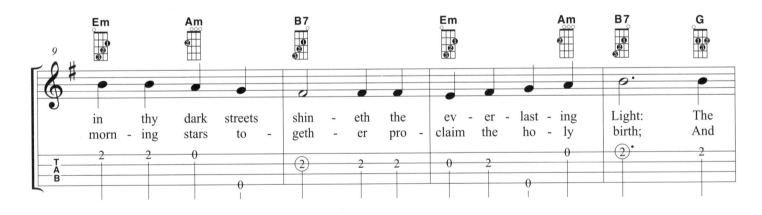

in thy dark streets shin - eth the ev - er - last - ing Light: The
morn - ing stars to - geth - er pro - claim the ho - ly birth; And

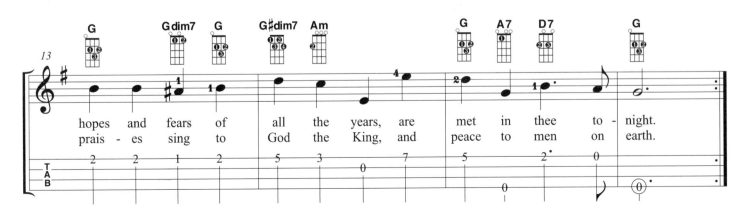

hopes and fears of all the years, are met in thee to - night.
prais - es sing to God the King, and peace to men on earth.

G1074

Once in David's Royal City

Lyrics by Cecil Frances Alexander
Music by Henry John Gauntlett

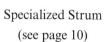

Over the River and Through the Wood

Lyrics by Lydia Maria Child
Traditional Melody

PARADE OF THE WOODEN SOLDIERS

MUSIC BY LEON JESSEL

Specialized Strum
(see page 10)

Join the march!

RING LITTLE BELLS

TRADITIONAL GERMAN CAROL

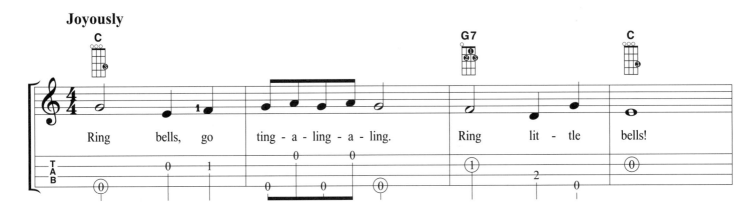

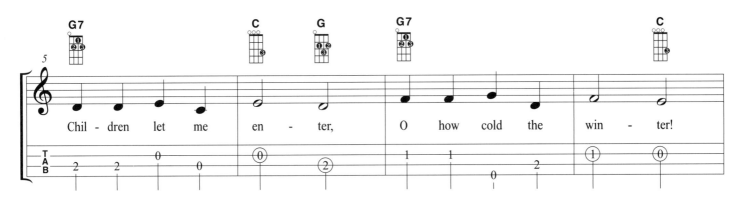

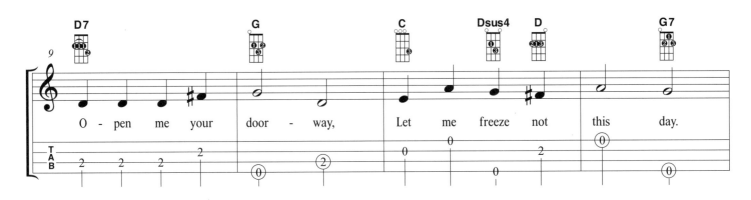

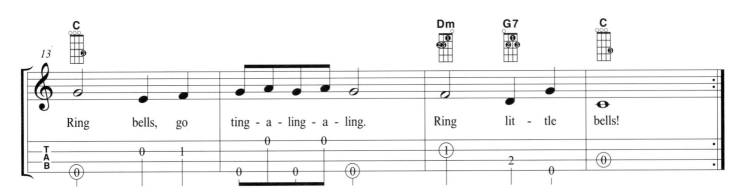

ROCKING CAROL

HAJEJ, NYNEJ, JEZISKU
TRADITIONAL CZECH CAROL

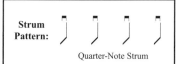

SILENT NIGHT

STILLE NACHT

LYRICS BY JOSEPH MOHR
MUSIC BY FRANZ GRUBER

SING WE NOW OF CHRISTMAS

NOËL NOUVELET

TRADITIONAL FRENCH CAROL

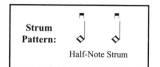

Strum Pattern:
Half-Note Strum

Moderately

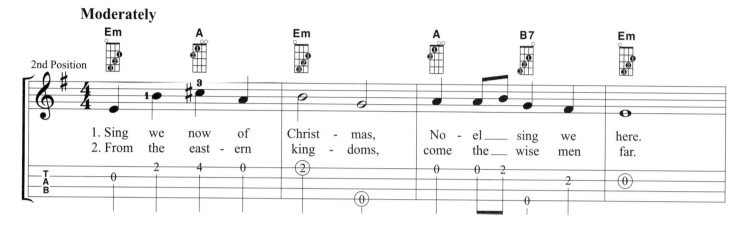

2nd Position

1. Sing we now of Christ - mas, No - el___ sing we here.
2. From the east - ern king - doms, come the___ wise men here far.

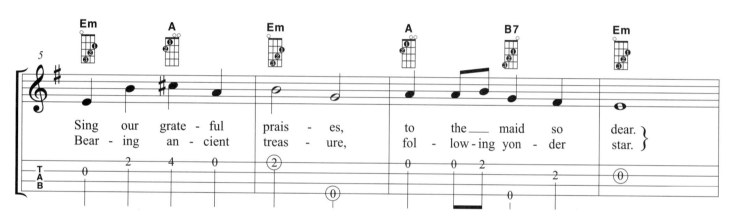

Sing our grate - ful prais - es, to the___ maid so dear. }
Bear - ing an - cient treas - ure, fol - low-ing yon - der star. }

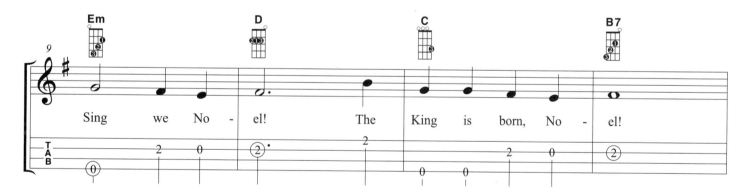

Sing we No - el! The King is born, No - el!

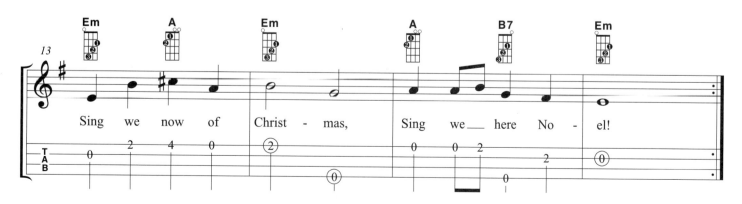

Sing we now of Christ - mas, Sing we___ here No - el!

SKATERS' WALTZ

LES PATINEURS VALSE

ÉMILE WALDTEUFEL

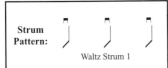

TOYLAND

LYRICS BY GLEN MACDONOUGH
MUSIC BY VICTOR HERBERT

THE TWELVE DAYS OF CHRISTMAS
OLD ENGLISH CAROL

Specialized Strum
(see page 10)

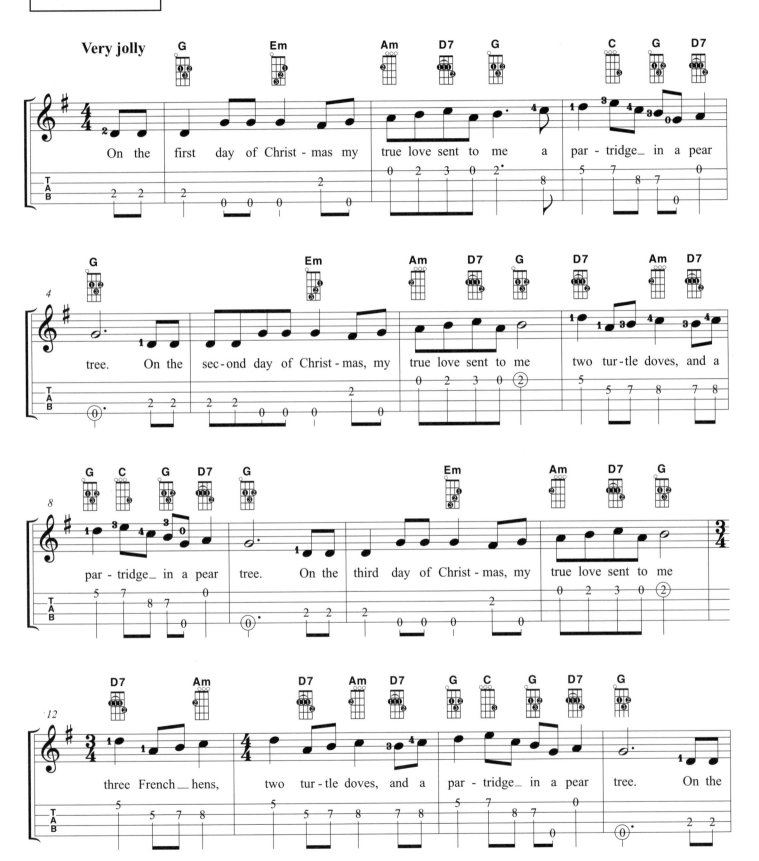

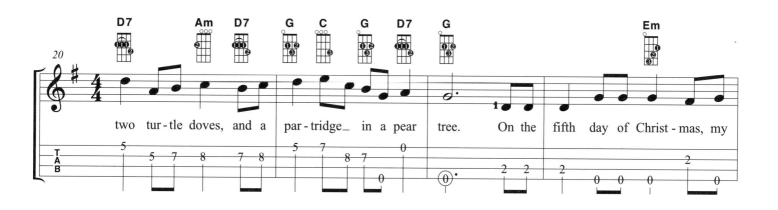

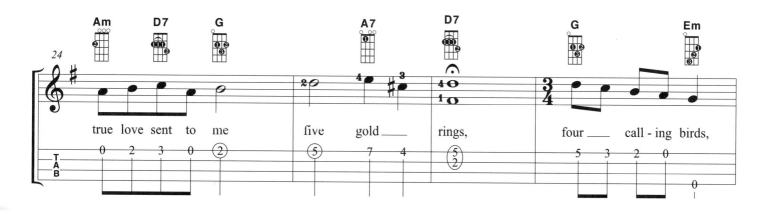

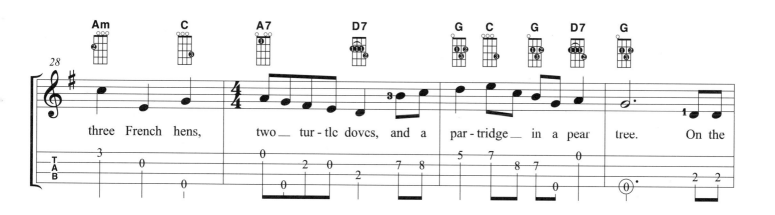

Repeat as needed.

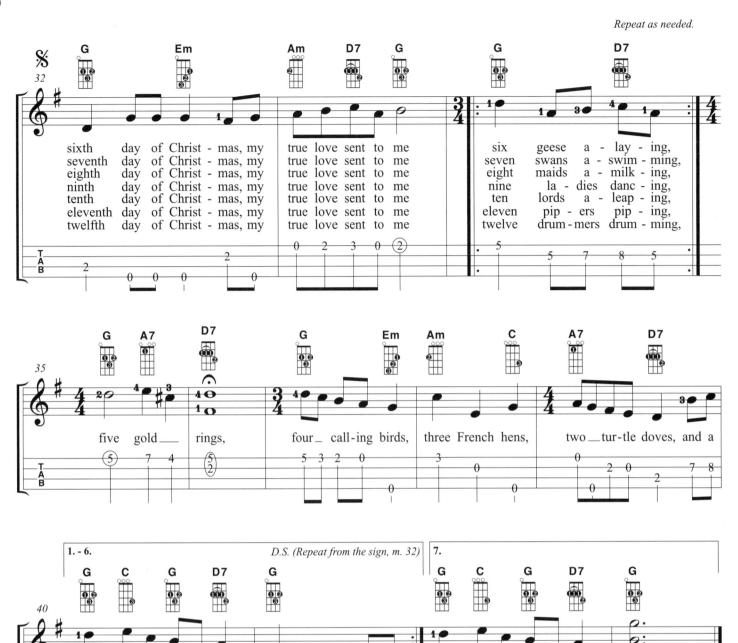

Up on the Housetop

Lyrics and Music by Benjamin R. Hanby

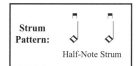

Ukrainian Bell Carol

Adapted by Mykola D. Leontovych

* hammer-on

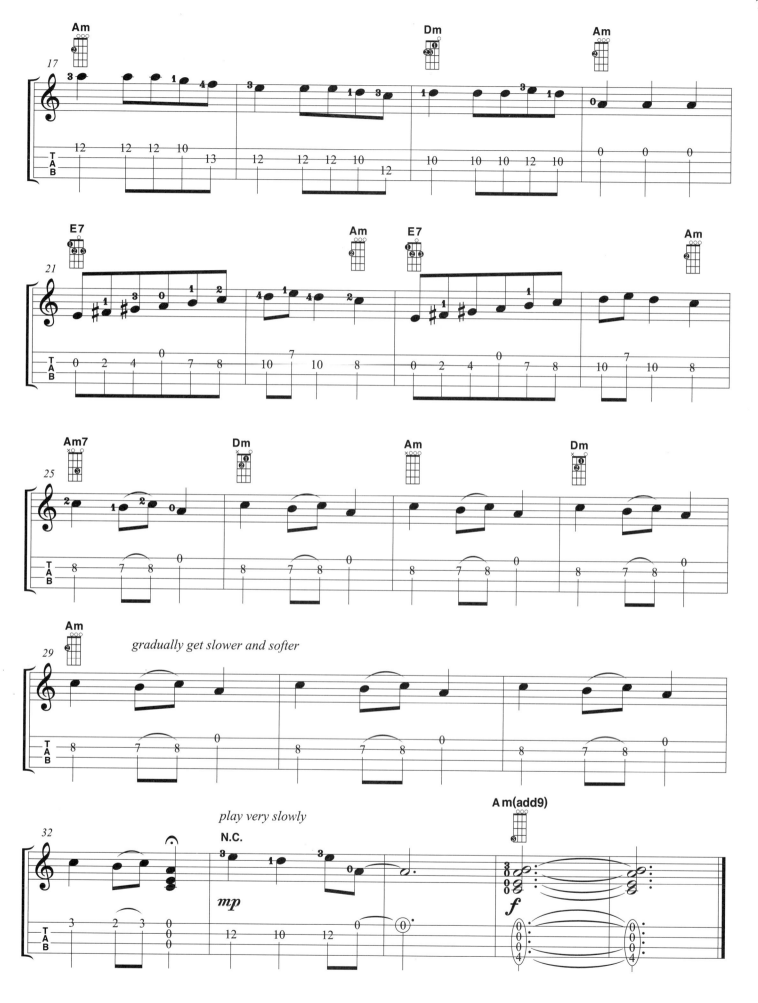

We Three Kings of Orient Are

Lyrics and Music by John H. Hopkins Jr.

We Wish You a Merry Christmas

Traditional English Carol

What Child Is This

Greensleeves

Lyrics by William Chatterly Dix
Traditional English Melody

Strum Pattern: Waltz Folk Strum 3

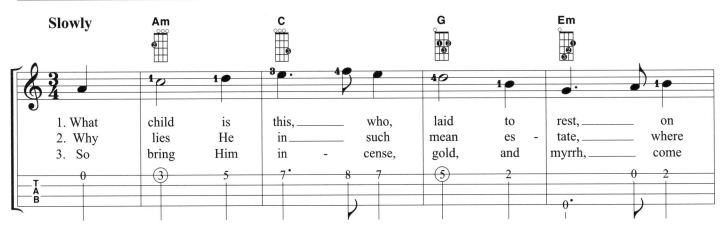

Slowly

1. What child is this, who, laid to rest, on
2. Why lies He in such mean es - tate, where
3. So bring Him in - cense, gold, and myrrh, come

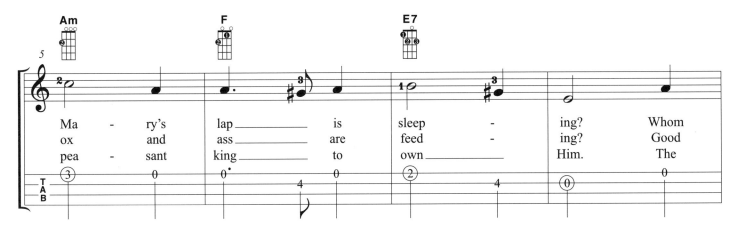

Ma - ry's lap is sleep - ing? Whom
ox and ass are feed - ing? Good
pea - sant king to own Him. The

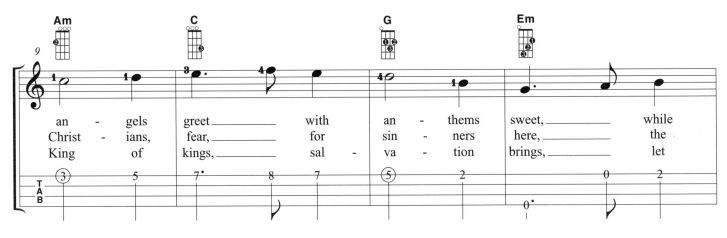

an - gels greet with an - thems sweet, while
Christ - ians, fear, with for sin - ners here, the
King of kings, sal - va - tion brings, let

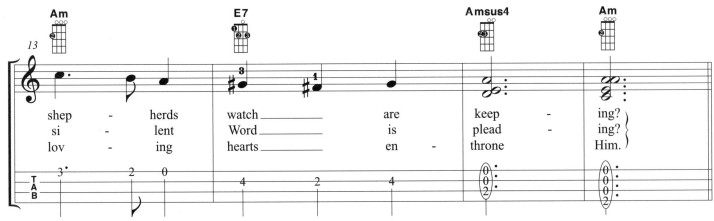

shep - herds watch are keep - ing?
si - lent Word is plead - ing?
lov - ing hearts en - throne Him.

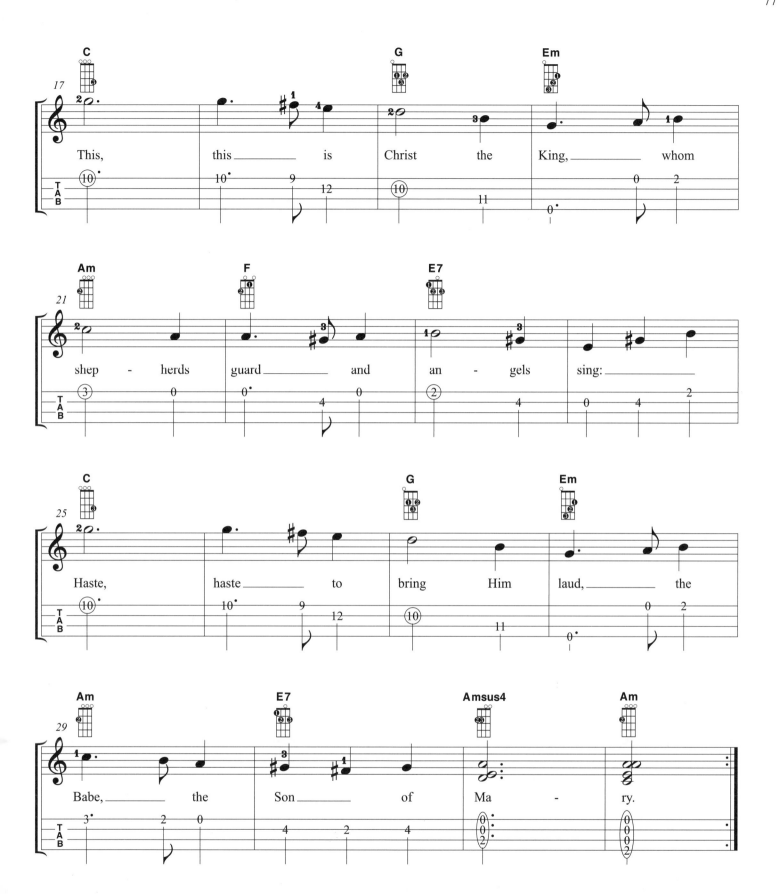

Wexford Carol

Traditional Irish Carol

Specialized Strum
(see page 10)

WHILE SHEPHERDS WATCHED THEIR FLOCKS BY NIGHT

MEDLEY

LYRICS BY NAHUM TATE/MUSIC: THE WHOLE BOOKE OF PSALMES; GEORGE FRIDERIC HANDEL

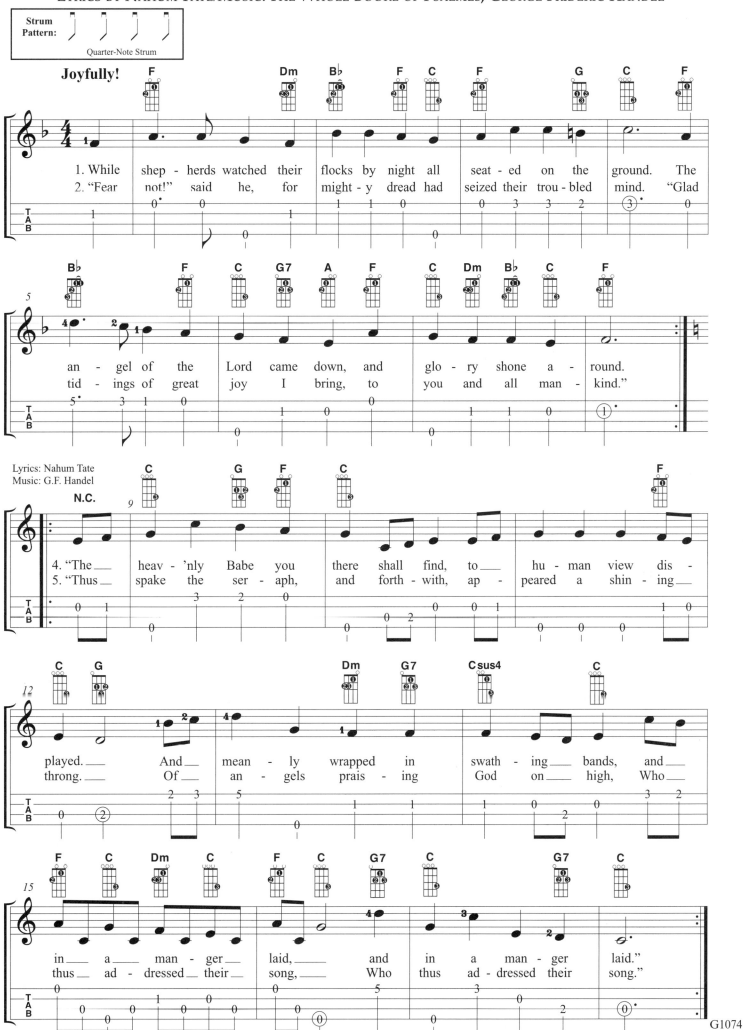

Glossary

a tempo   indicates to return to the previous tempo after a *ritardando* (*ritard.*)

Chorus   the part of a song that occurs after each verse, and uses the same words. It is also known as the *Refrain*.

dynamics   the loudness or softness of the music: *f* (*forte*, loud); *mf* (*mezzo forte*, medium loud); *mp* (*mezzo piano*, medium soft); *p* (*piano*, soft). If there is not a dynamic indication, play *mf*.

hammer on   a guitar technique used on ascending notes. A slur indicates that the first note is picked with the right hand but the second note is sounded by a left-hand finger descending down on the note without any use of the right hand.

key signature   the sharps or flats at the beginning of each line of music that indicates the key of the piece. Some examples are: Key of C (no sharps or flats); Key of G (one sharp); Key of D (two sharps); Key of F (one flat).

N.C.   (No Chord) indicates that the rhythm (chords) stops playing while the melody continues

pick-up notes   occur when the music does not start on beat 1

position playing   a ukulele technique where the fretting hand is placed in a fixed position and each finger is assigned to a certain fret. For example, in Second Position, the 1st finger plays the notes on the 2nd fret, the 2nd finger plays the notes on the 3rd fret, the 3rd finger plays the notes on the 4th fret, and the 4th finger plays the notes on the 5th fret. Positions 2 and higher usually do not contain any open strings.

ritard.   an abbreviation for *ritardando*. Gradually get slower.

swing rhythm   play eighth notes as a "long-short" pattern rather than playing all eighth notes equally

tempo   term that appears at the beginning of a song that lets the performer know how fast or slow the song is to be

time signature   two numbers placed at the beginning of a piece that indicate the meter. The top number indicates the amount of beats in one measure and the bottom number (usually a 4 or 8) indicates what type of note receives one beat. The bottom 4 indicates that a quarter note receives one beat and the bottom 8 indicates that an eighth note receives one beat. This book uses four different time signatures: 4/4, 3/4, 2/4, and 6/8.

tremolo   the repetition of a note or chord using rapid down and upstrokes (≋)

triplets   a note value where three notes are played in the time value of two notes. Eighth-note triplets are three notes played on one beat.

Verse   the part of a song that uses different words each time it is sung, also known as a *Stanza*